TABLE OF CONTENTS

Introduction to Coding

Coding

Coding, also referred to as programming, is creating instructions that can be executed on a computer to perform a specific task or achieve a particular result. Coding is just like solving a math problem. There may be many ways to solve a problem.

Language is our primary means of Communication for all human interactions. Similarly, we can interact with computers via a language that computers understand. This language is called a programming language.

Syntax

Syntax is a set of rules that we need to follow when we write a computer program. Every programming language has its own syntax. But all programming languages have one common thing: they are eventually converted into a language that the computer will understand.

Block Coding

Block coding refers to a method of organizing and writing computer programs by grouping instructions into "blocks" or sections of code. Each block typically performs a specific task or function. This approach helps make the code more organized, easier to understand, and modular, as different blocks can be reused in various parts of the program. Block coding is often used in visual programming environments or in languages that support modular programming practices. It simplifies the coding process and promotes better code structure.

Some of the Programming Languages are:
Python, Java, C, C++, R JavaScript, C#, Pearl, COBOL, HTML, php, Ruby, etc.

Game Development Basics with MakeCode Arcade

MakeCode Arcade is a free and user-friendly platform that allows you to create your own video games. It provides a simplified approach to coding and game development, making it accessible to beginners and experienced programmers alike. With MakeCode Arcade, you can unleash your creativity and bring your game ideas to life.

Getting Started with MakeCode Arcade

To get started with MakeCode Arcade, you can visit the official MakeCode website and click on the New" option. From there, you can either start a new project or explore existing games created by the community.

Understanding the MakeCode Arcade Interface

Once you've opened MakeCode Arcade, you'll notice a series of components that make up the interface. Let's take a closer look at each of these components:

Code Editor: This is where you'll write your game's code using block-based programming.

Sprite Editor: It allows you to create and customize the appearance of your game's characters or objects, known as sprites.

Scene Editor: It enables you to design the layout of your game's levels or screens.

Game Simulator: It provides a preview of your game in real-time. It allows you to test and play your game as you develop it, making it easier to identify and fix any issues.

MakeCode Arcade home page

Website Link : https://arcade.makecode.com/

Import a Project

Getting familiar with MakeCode Arcade

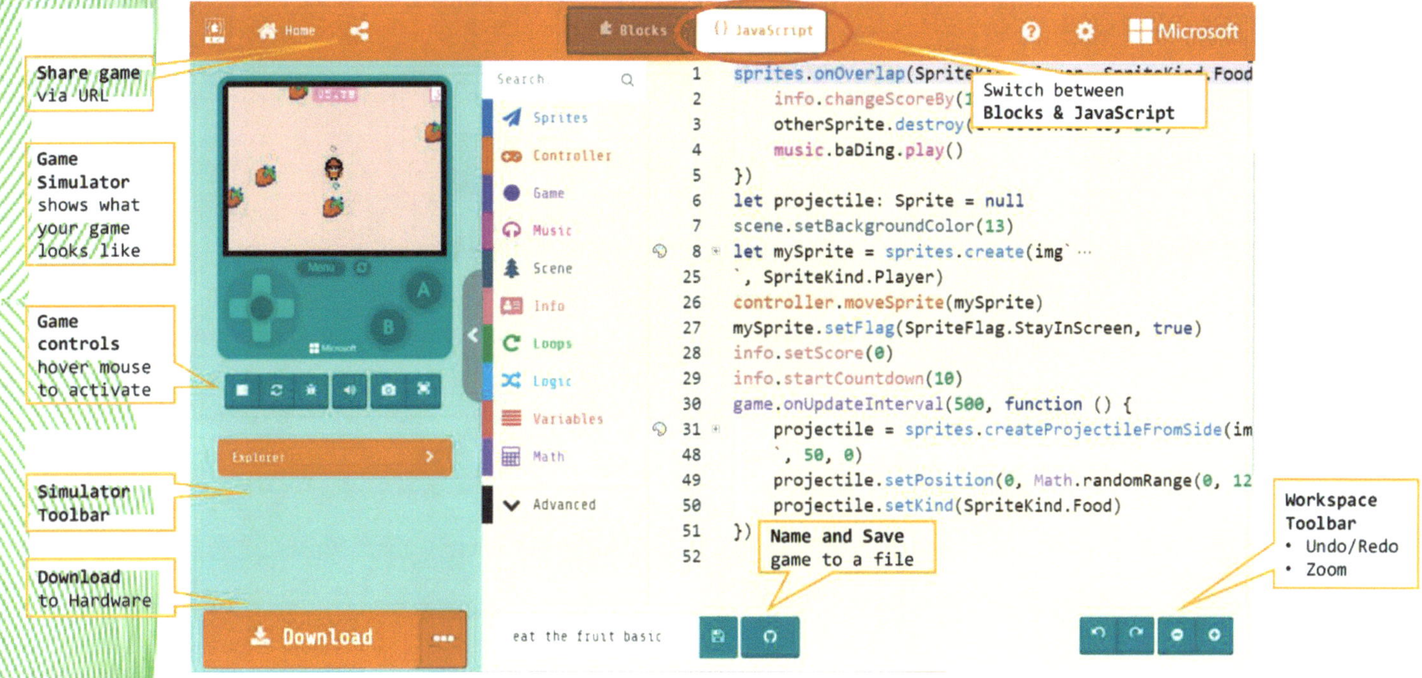

Share your game!

Click the Share button in the top left of the screen

Choosing Background

on start
set background image to

Choosing Background Color

on start
set background color to

Choosing Sprite

on start
set mySprite to sprite of kind Player

Setting up Position of Sprite

on start
set mySprite to sprite of kind Player
set mySprite position to x 0 y 0

x 0

x=82 y=103

Making video games is like creating art. Game developers have special rules they follow to make sure their games are good and liked by people. The world of video games is very competitive, but if you really love making games, it can lead to great job opportunities. Designing a fancy and easy-to-use game takes a lot of time and effort, including doing research. You also need to follow certain rules to make sure your games are loved by many people.

The
Realm of
Game Creation

DESIGN GAME PRINCIPLES

1. Making the Game Fun:

Think About Players: Games are made with players in mind. Creators try to understand what players like and make games that are enjoyable for them.

Balancing Fun and Challenge: Games need to be interesting but not too hard. If a game is just the right amount of challenging, it's more fun for players.

Clear Goals and Progress: Games should have clear goals so players know what they're supposed to do. Getting feedback on how well they're doing keeps players motivated.

2. Tech Stuff:

Works Everywhere: Games should work on different devices like phones or computers. This way, everyone can play.

Runs Smoothly: Creators make sure the game doesn't freeze or have problems while people are playing. This makes for a better experience.

3. Making Things Look Good:

Nice to Look At: Games should look good and have a consistent style.

Easy to Use Menus: The buttons and menus in a game should be easy to understand. This helps players move around the game without getting confused.

4. Telling a Story:

Interesting Story: Games with cool stories and characters are more fun. It's like being part of an exciting adventure.

Player Choices Matter: Games where players can make choices that affect the story make the game more interesting.

5. Testing and Improving:

Ask Players for Help: Creators ask people to play the game and tell them what they like or don't like. This helps make the game better.

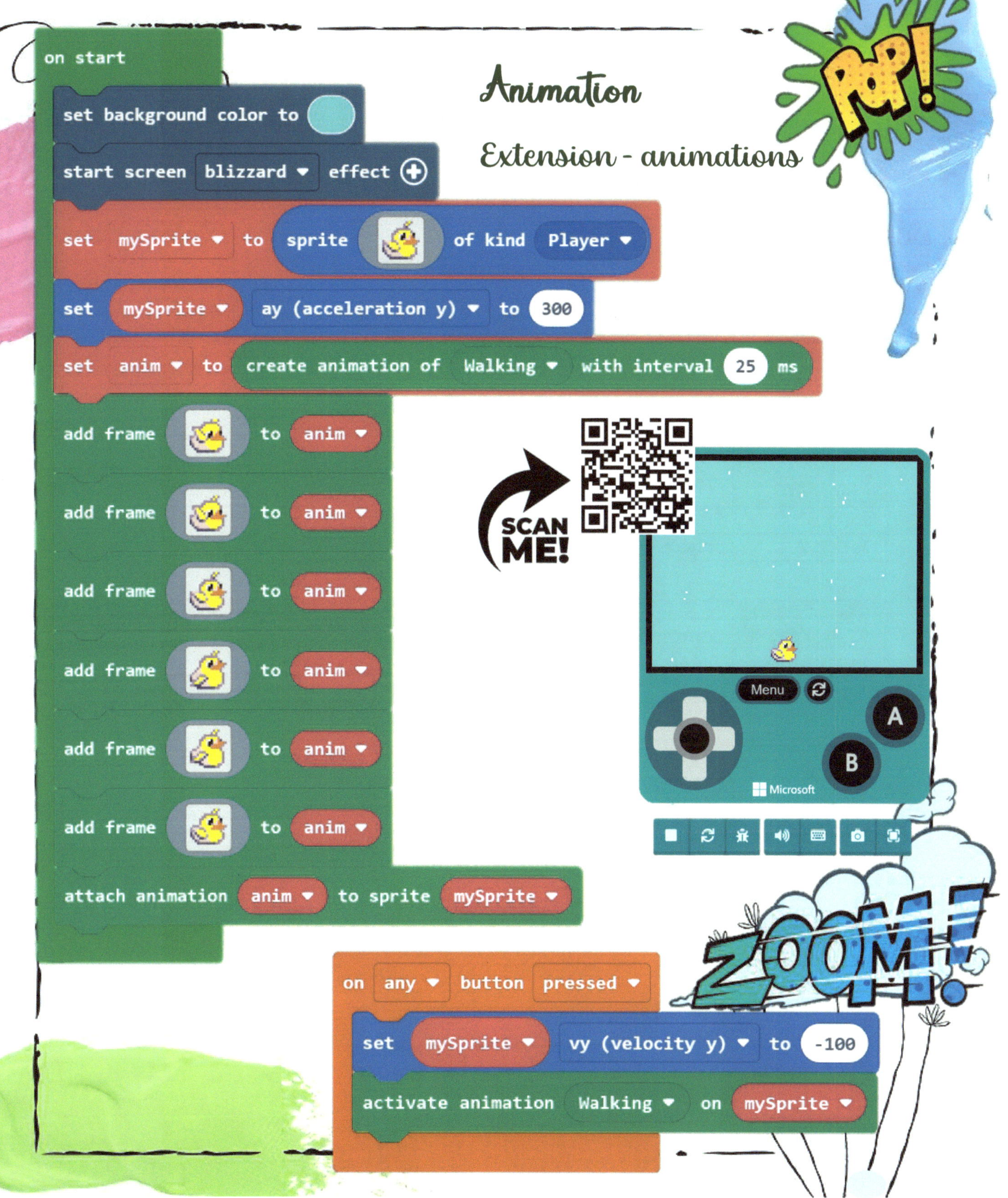
Animation
Extension - animations
POP!
on start
set background color to
start screen blizzard effect
set mySprite to sprite of kind Player
set mySprite ay (acceleration y) to 300
set anim to create animation of Walking with interval 25 ms
add frame to anim
add frame to anim
add frame to anim
add frame to anim
add frame to anim
add frame to anim
attach animation anim to sprite mySprite
SCAN ME!
Menu
A
B
Microsoft
ZOOM!
on any button pressed
set mySprite vy (velocity y) to -100
activate animation Walking on mySprite

MCQ

Question 1	For a given problem, there is always only one way to write a program
Option 1	True
Option 2	False

Question 2	Pin authentication for ATM card transaction is an example of programming
Option 1	True
Option 2	False

Question 3	Code is a set of instructions that can be executed on a computer to perform a specific task
Option 1	True
Option 2	False

Question 4	Which among the below are examples of programming in real life?
Option 1	Robots
Option 2	Computer Games
Option 3	Self-drive cars
Option 4	All the above

Question 5	Which among the below is not an example of programming language?
Option 1	Python
Option 2	English
Option 3	JavaScript

Fun With Variables

Fun With Variables

Variables

In programming, variable is a packet in which we can store data. These packets can be named and referenced and can be used to perform various operations. To perform a mathematical operation, you can declare two variables and perform the operation on them

Scope

Scope of a variable refers to the part of the code where the variable can be used. The scope of the variables defined in a program depends on where you have declared it in each program. Any defined variable cannot be accessed beyond its scope

Naming & Datatypes

Every variable in a program is unique. This name acts as an identifier for that variable. In programming, a user is not allowed to use the same name of a variable more than once. If variable named as "a" is equal to 2 and variable named as "b" is equal to 2, performing add operation on "a" and "b" is going to result into an output as "4".

Every value needs to be assigned to a specific data type to make the variable more readable by a computer.

Data type identifies what the type of data that the declared variable can hold is. Thus, it indirectly helps the computer to understand what operations need to be performed on those variables. The declaration of a variable in a program contains two components – the name of the variable and its type.

Let us now understand what are the common data types that we can use in programming:

- Integer
- Floating-point number
- String
- Boolean

Integer data type variables store integer values only. They store whole numbers which have zero, positive and negative values but not decimal values. Example : a = 1

Floating-point numbers are used to store decimal values. They hold real numbers with decimal values. Example : a = 1.1

Boolean is a subtype of integer data type. It stores true and false where true means non-zero and false means zero. Example : a= true

A user may have a requirement to store and perform an operation on a sequence of characters. In such cases, the String data type is present to fit the gap. Example : a=" Hello"

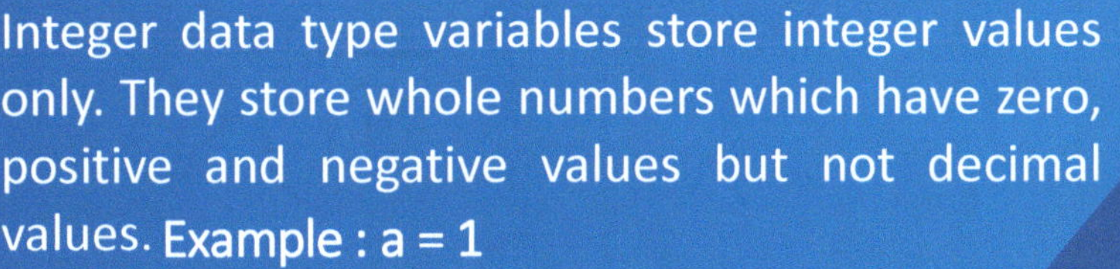

Rules for naming a variable:

- A variable name cannot start with a number, it must start with an alphabet or underscore (_) sign
- Variable name is case sensitive. Sum and sum are different variables
- A variable can only contain alpha numeric characters and underscore

Morphing Effect

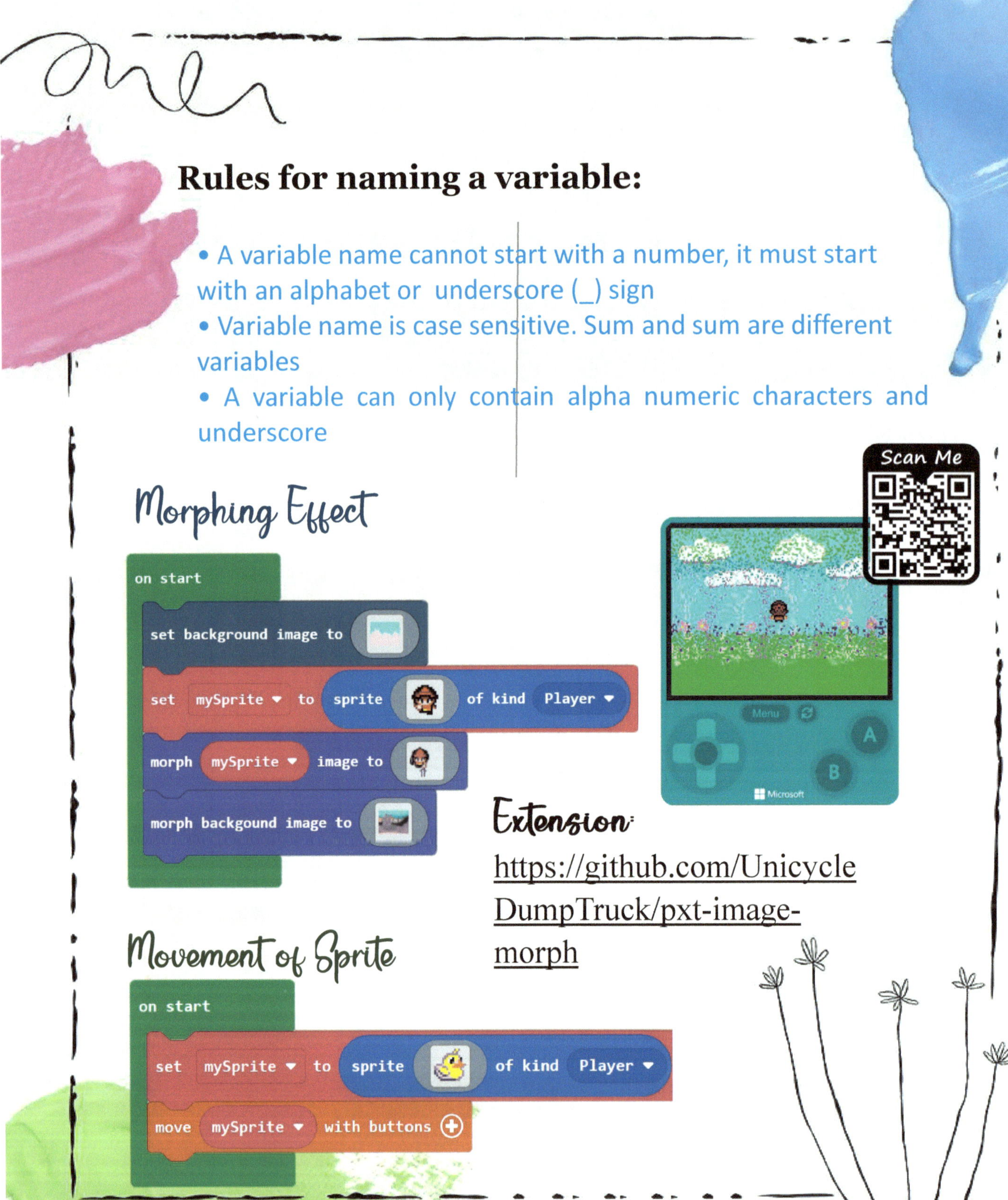

Extension:

https://github.com/Unicycle DumpTruck/pxt-image-morph

Movement of Sprite

Character Animation

Extension:

riknoll/character-animations

Adding Clock

Extension:

https://blobbey2000.github.io/pxt-clock/ & Story telling

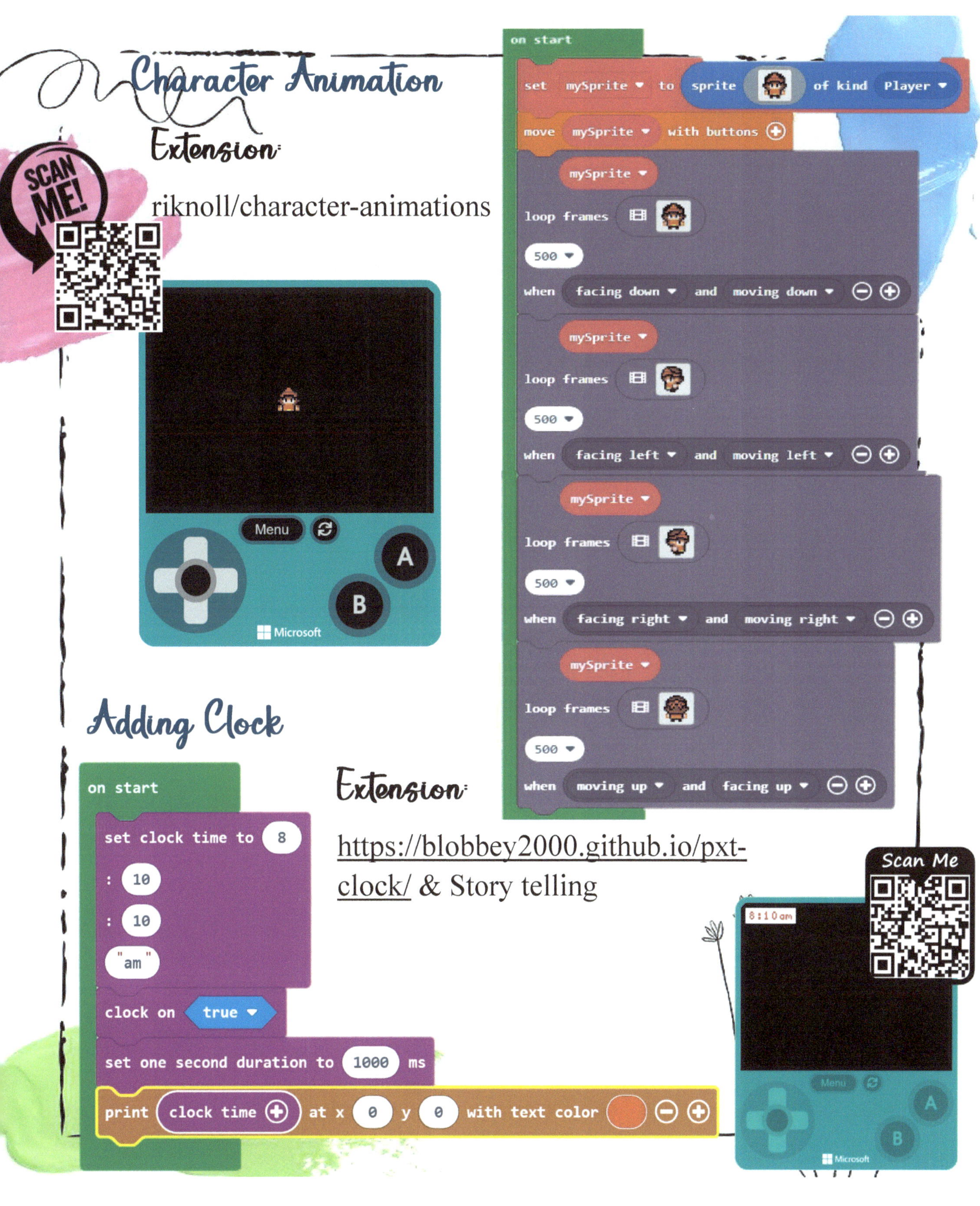

True/False Questions:

1. The data type of a variable influences the kind of operations that can be performed on it.

2. Variable names in programming can include spaces for better readability.

3. The variable "Sum" and "sum" are considered the same in programming.

4. The data type of a variable must be explicitly declared during its usage in programming.

Fill in the Blanks:

1. The ______________ of a variable is the part of the code where the variable can be used.

2. Every variable in a program must be assigned a specific ______________ to make it more readable for the computer.

3. Example: a = "Hello" demonstrates the usage of the ______________ data type.

4. A variable name cannot start with a ______________, it must start with an alphabet or underscore () sign.

Short Questions-

1. Define variables in programming
2. Can we declare two variables in a program with the same name? Justify your answer.
3. What are the common Data Types in programming?
4. What is the scope of a variable?
5. How we be able to know the data type of a variable?

Control With Conditions

Control With Conditions

Logical Operators

Logical operators are fundamental blocks that can be used to build a decision-making capability in your code.

The three most important logical operators are AND, OR and NOT.

Relational Operators

Operator	Symbol	Example	Meaning
Greater than	>	x > y	x greater than y
Equal to	==	x == y	x is equal to y
Less than	<	x < y	x is less than y
Greater than or equal to	>=	x >= y	x is either greater than or equal to y
Less than or equal to	<=	x <= y	x is either less than or equal to y
Not equal to	!=	x! = y	x is not equal to y

Reminders

- Condition 1: Have you completed homework?
- Condition 2: Is the time past 8 PM?
- And the decision we are deriving is:
- Decision: Should you go to bed? Based on this we can write the below pseudo code:

IF (Homework completed) **AND** (Time is past 8 PM) :

    Go to bed

ELSE :

    Do not go to bed

Pixel Overlap

```
on start
set mySprite ▼ to sprite (○) of kind Player ▼
set mySprite2 ▼ to sprite (▲) of kind Player ▼
move mySprite2 ▼ with buttons ⊕

on game update
if ( mySprite ▼ overlaps with mySprite2 ▼ ) then
    set background color to
else
    set background color to
```

Rain Effect
Hopping
SCAN ME!
SCAN ME!
Menu
A
B
Microsoft
forever
set mySprite to sprite 1 of kind rain
set mySprite position to x pick random -300 to 300 y pick random -300 to 160
set mySprite vy (velocity y) to 150
on start
set background image to
set mySprite to sprite of kind Player
set mySprite position to x 16 y 96
on A button pressed
set mySprite vy (velocity y) to -200
play sound ba ding until done
on game update
if mySprite y < 96 then
set mySprite ay (acceleration y) to 350
else
set mySprite ay (acceleration y) to 0
set mySprite vy (velocity y) to 0

True/False -

1. The NOT operator in logical operations negates the value of a condition.

2. The XOR operator returns true if both conditions are true.

3. Logical operators are essential only for building loops in code.

4. The ELSE statement in the provided pseudo code is executed when the IF condition is true.

Fill in the blanks -

1. Logical operators are fundamental blocks that help in building a ______________ capability in code.

2. The three most important logical operators are ______________, ______________, and ______________.

3. In the provided pseudo code, if the conditions "Homework completed" and "Time is past 8 PM" are both true, the decision is to ______________.

4. The decision-making structure in the provided pseudo code is an example of an ______________ statement.

Short Questions-

1. What are the different types of logical operators? Explain with examples.
2. Explain with example on how to combine different logical operators.
3. What are the different types of relational operators?
4. Write the code to create snow effect.

LOOPS
USING BLOCKS
Nintendo GAME BOY
SELECT
START
PHONES

Loops Using Blocks

Loops

In programming, repetition of a line or a block of code is also known as iteration. A loop is an algorithm which executes a block of code multiple times till the time a specified condition is met. Therefore, we can say that a loop iterates a block of code multiple times till the time mentioned condition is satisfied.

Below are the two important benefits of loops:

1. Reduces lines of code
2. Code becomes easier to understand

Types

Loops make our code more manageable and organized. The different types of loops are:

1. While Loop
2. For Loop
3. Nested Loop

The While Loop The While loop can execute a set of commands till the condition is true While Loops are also called conditional loops. Once the condition is met then the loop is finished.

Example 1 – Print number from 1 to 15 Here, if we want to derive the loop from this scenario
Condition: Write from 1 to 15 And the decision we are deriving is:
Decision: Have we reached 15

Reminders

Execution of loops is based on iterations. To run a block of code in a loop, one needs to set a condition and set its number of iterations. Each time the condition is true, and the block of code executes once, it is counted to be one iteration. Before moving to the next iteration, one needs to increase the count of iteration to two. This is called as incrementing a loop.

The For Loop For loop is needed for iterating over a sequence. A for loop executes for a specific number of times.

```
for i in range(5)
    print("I will study every day.")
    i++
```

Adding Music

SCAN ME!

2 D Maze

on start
set mySprite to sprite of kind Player
set tilemap to tilemap
move mySprite with buttons
camera follow sprite mySprite
place mySprite on top of random

Menu
A
B
Microsoft

Scan me!!

Monkey Eating Fruit

on start
set mySprite to sprite of kind Player
move mySprite with buttons
start countdown 10 (s)
set background image to

on game update every 500 ms
set projectile to projectile from side with vx pick random -50

on sprite of kind Player overlaps otherSprite of kind Projectile
destroy otherSprite with halo effect for 500 ms
play sound pew pew until done
change score by 1

05.79

Menu
A
B
Microsoft

True/False Questions:

1. Repetition of a line or block of code in programming is known as recursion.

2. A loop in programming executes a block of code a specific number of times until a specified condition is met.

3. One of the benefits of using loops is that they increase the number of lines of code in a program.

4. The execution of loops is based on conditions, and each execution of the loop is referred to as an iteration.

Fill in the Blanks:

1. To run a block of code in a loop, one needs to set a _____________ and specify its number of _____________.

2. The For Loop is particularly useful for iterating over a _____________.

3. A While Loop can be considered a _____________ loop, as it executes as long as a specified condition is true.

4. Incrementing a loop involves increasing the count of _____________ before moving to the next iteration.

Short Questions-

1. Explain for loop and while loop with example.
2. Write two benefits of using loops?
3. How do we increment loops?
4. Write the code in which as you move the camera should also move?

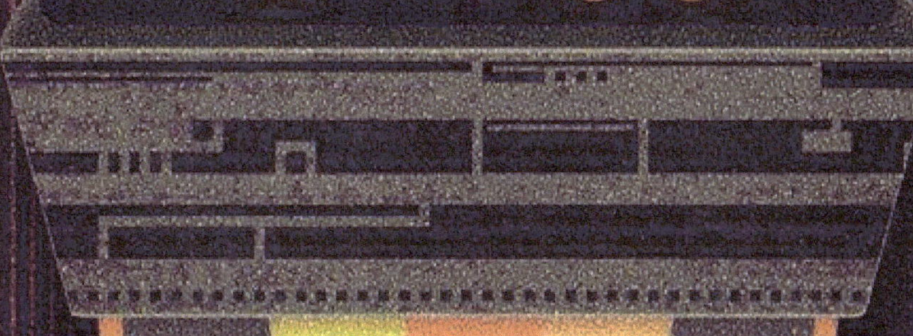

BACKDROPS
Structures
Using Blocks

Structures Using Blocks

Entry Criteria

Entry criteria is defined as a condition that must be met before starting a specific task. It is a set of conditions that must exist before you can start a task. These criteria differ from program to program as per the requirement.

For example, To start a car you need petrol/diesel. If your fuel tank is empty your car won't start. So, the entry criteria for the car to start is fuel tank should not be empty.

Exit Criteria

Exit criteria is defined as a condition that must be met before completing a specific task. It is a set of conditions that must exist before you can declare a program to be complete. Without an exit criterion, the program tends to enter in an infinite loop.

Break & Continue

The break statement modifies the normal flow of execution while it terminates the existing loop and continues execution of the statement following that loop. Break statement is required as sometimes you want to break out of a loop early when a condition is met.

Whenever a program comes across a continue statement, the control skips the execution of remaining statements inside the loop for the current iteration and jumps to the beginning of the loop for the next iteration. If the loop's condition is still true, it enters the loop again, else the control will be moved to the statement immediately after the loop. This is somewhat similar to break statement and is used when we want to force the next iteration and skip some lines of code within the loop.

3 D Maze

Extension – raycasting

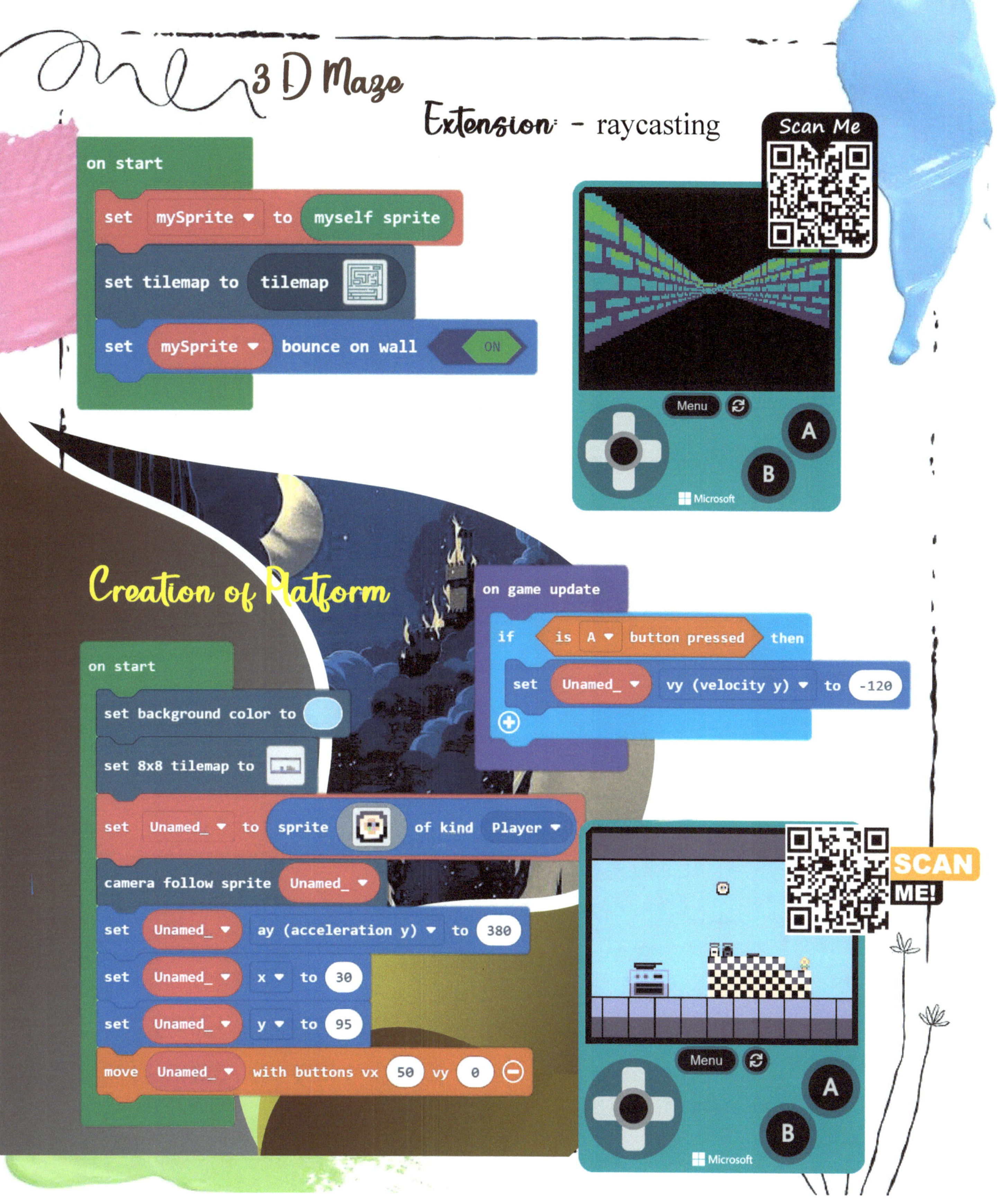

Creation of Tile Map
on start
set tilemap to tilemap
set background image to
on menu button pressed
toggle current view mode
Menu
A
B
Microsoft
SCAN
ME!

True/False Questions:

1. The break statement is used to terminate a loop and continue with the next iteration.

2. An entry criterion for starting a car might include having the radio turned on.

3. The continue statement is used to terminate the loop early when a condition is met.

Fill in the Blanks:

1. Entry criteria for a task are the conditions that must be met before ______________ a specific task.

2. The break statement is used to modify the normal flow of execution and terminate the existing ______________.

3. The continue statement is used to skip the execution of remaining statements inside the loop for the current iteration and jump to the ______________.

Short Questions-

1. Write the extension to create 3D Maze?
2. What is an exit and entry criterion?
3. What is a break statement?
4. What is the use of velocity in block coding?
5. What is a continue statement?

Capstone Project

PROJECT NAME: _______________________

SCHOOL NAME: _______________________

YEAR/CLASS: _______________________

TEACHER NAME: _______________________

TEAM MEMBER NAMES

1. _______________________

2. _______________________

3. _______________________

4. _______________________

5. _______________________

Phase 1: Idea Generation

Individual MVP Game Development:
Each team member develops the game ideas independently.
Encourage creativity and variety to explore diverse concepts.

____

____

____

____

____

Phase 2: Team Roles

2.1 Who is in your team and what are their roles?

Role	Role description	Team Member Name

Phase 3: Group Discussion

1. Group Meeting:

- Schedule a meeting to discuss individual MVP games.
- Identify strengths, weaknesses, and innovative elements of each game.

2.Consolidation:

- Combine the most promising aspects from each MVP game into a list.
- Decide on the core theme and features for the final project.

Phase 4: Final Game Development

Individual Task Completion:
Have each team member focus on completing their assigned tasks.

Enter the URL of your team's game: